TYSON HANSEN

Why Young Adults Struggle Financially

The Condensed Explanation of the Looming Financial Struggles Faced Today and How to Overcome Them

Copyright © 2024 by Tyson Hansen

All rights reserved. No part of this publication may be reproduced, stored or transmitted in any form or by any means, electronic, mechanical, photocopying, recording, scanning, or otherwise without written permission from the publisher. It is illegal to copy this book, post it to a website, or distribute it by any other means without permission.

Tyson Hansen asserts the moral right to be identified as the author of this work.

Tyson Hansen has no responsibility for the persistence or accuracy of URLs for external or third-party Internet Websites referred to in this publication and does not guarantee that any content on such Websites is, or will remain, accurate or appropriate.

Designations used by companies to distinguish their products are often claimed as trademarks. All brand names and product names used in this book and on its cover are trade names, service marks, trademarks and registered trademarks of their respective owners. The publishers and the book are not associated with any product or vendor mentioned in this book. None of the companies referenced within the book have endorsed the book.

First edition

This book was professionally typeset on Reedsy.
Find out more at reedsy.com

Contents

1 Introduction 1
2 The Shortcomings of Education 3
3 Evolving Economics 9
4 Social and Political Pressure 14
5 The Way Out of Financial Despair 18
6 Conclusion 27
7 Resources 29

1

Introduction

You're standing at a crossroads—financially speaking. Each decision, each moment, shapes your economic future. This isn't just another book about money; it's your wake-up call. Your financial struggles, though daunting, aren't unique, and they're far from unbeatable. You're about to embark on a no-nonsense journey through the gritty reality of financial hardship facing young adults today. But more importantly, you'll discover proven strategies to overcome these challenges and forge a path to financial independence.

Why this book? Because too many young adults wander through their financial lives without a clue, caught in a cycle of debt, dissatisfaction, and despair. This book cuts through that noise. It offers a distilled, direct approach to understanding and conquering the economic forces at play. From the shortcomings in our education system that leave you unprepared, to the evolving economic landscapes that test your adaptability, to the social and political pressures that shape your financial decisions—this book covers it all.

As the author, I've witnessed these struggles firsthand and helped others navigate them. I'm not here to coddle you with comforting lies or empty reassurances. Instead, I offer you the tools and mindset necessary to take control of your financial destiny. By the end of this book, not only will you understand the root causes of your financial woes, but you'll also be equipped with the knowledge, tactics, and other suggested books to overcome them.

Expect hard truths and straightforward advice. Each chapter builds on the last, creating a comprehensive guide that will transform not just how you view money but how you manage it. You're not just reading for insight; you're preparing for action.

As we transition into the next chapter, remember this: the path to financial freedom is not paved with easy shortcuts or overnight success stories. It's built on hard work, intelligent decisions, and an unwavering commitment to self-improvement. Ready to get started? Let's explore the real reasons behind our educational system's financial shortcomings, setting the stage for a deeper understanding and a more robust financial foundation.

2

The Shortcomings of Education

Strike One: The Homefront Failure

According to a OnePoll survey, 59% of parents feel uncomfortable discussing finances with their kids! This survey included 2,000 parents.

The foundational lessons of financial management—earning, saving, and investing—are crucial yet often overlooked or inadequately addressed in many households. In some homes, parents diligently attempt to teach these principles. Still, the lessons may be brushed aside as young adults choose to ignore the advice given, often due to a lack of interest or understanding of its long-term importance. Conversely, some young adults might strive to understand and implement financial education, yet external economic challenges and personal financial crises render these lessons less effective or relevant in practice. This creates a situation where young adults remain in the comfort of their parent's homes without facing the financial pressures of adulthood. In fact, many young adults are allowed, even encouraged, to linger in their parents' basements, shielded from the economic realities of life. Consequently, this protective bubble delays financial independence and maturity, leaving many young adults unprepared to handle real-world financial responsibilities. The problem is twofold: not only the absence of financial teachings but also the failure to engage with and apply such teachings effectively.

How did this become such a pandemic? Unfortunately, there is no definite starting point, and there does not seem to be an end. Going back to the OnePoll survey, 83% of those parents wished they had been taught more about finances with 13% saying that money was never brought up to them by their parents. It isn't any wonder why 59% of parents don't feel comfortable talking about finances to their kids. They didn't learn about it either, and the issue keeps rippling from generation to generation. However, uncomfortable or not, more parents, 82%, are looking for ways to teach their children about finances.

I don't recall any specific time when my parents sat me down and talked to me about money. It probably happened. What I do remember is them being an example by being money conscientious when making spending decisions. Also, they made sure that we knew how to work, and in return, we would receive an allowance when we were younger and actual hourly wages when we got into our teens. If we wanted something, it was up to us to purchase it with our own money…for the most part. If we ran out of money, we didn't get what we wanted. It didn't take long to catch on when we didn't eat for three days because we spent our money on toys and other non-essential items. Alright, so having to buy our own food isn't necessarily true, but we did learn how to manage our finances better.

As you will see in the next chapter, external economic challenges significantly compound these educational gaps, underscoring the complexity of today's youth's financial literacy crisis. But first, we need to confront strike number two in the educational shortcomings.

Strike Two: The Educational System's Miss

Student loan debt is $1.77 trillion in the United States alone or an average of $38,000 per borrower.

While schools are tasked with preparing students for real life, they significantly fall short in teaching one of the most crucial life skills: financial management. Even basic concepts like budgeting, managing debts, or understanding credit are not staples of the typical curriculum. The reasons for this gap are multifaceted. Primarily, there is a historical emphasis on traditional academic subjects—math, science, and history—that are deemed essential for standardized testing and college preparation. Financial education often does not fit neatly into these categories, and thus, it is not prioritized. Furthermore, there is a lack of qualified educators who are trained to teach personal finance effectively. The bureaucracy of educational systems also plays a role, where curriculum changes are slow and often meet resistance when it comes to integrating new and practical subjects.

Ironically, as the need for such education becomes more critical, the cost of schooling itself is escalating. After all, schools, like any other business, want to make a profit. Higher education, in particular, has seen tuition fees skyrocket, plunging students into significant debt before they even enter the workforce. This trend exacerbates the financial illiteracy problem—students are expected to manage substantial loans without the requisite knowledge to do so effectively. The rising education costs highlight a cruel irony: while students pay more for their education, they are often left with a gap in one of the most essential life skills—financial literacy. This systemic failure in the educational system not only undermines the economic stability of young adults but also limits their potential for financial independence and success.

Two weeks. That's it. I was taught the basics of managing a checkbook (a written log of any income and expenses for any millennials or Gen Zers reading this) in junior high for two weeks. It wasn't until college that I took a Finance 101 course. Was it required? Nope. It was one of the most eye-opening courses I took, and I have reflected on it many times since. It almost exceeds the natural disasters course that I was required to take. I've used that knowledge nearly every day of my life…if only if only. Although the course was interesting yet, at the same time, boring, it has not influenced any major or even minor decisions in my life. I get that we should be well-rounded in our knowledge, but it boggles my mind that finances aren't a part of that process.

There are silver linings. In 2023, 40.5% of high schoolers were required to take a finance course, according to Next Gen Personal Finance, a nonprofit helping to put finance resources in schools. This is up from 22.7% in 2022.

Strike Three: Self-Education Slip-ups

THE SHORTCOMINGS OF EDUCATION

Despite the gaps in formal education, many young adults take the initiative to self-educate on financial matters. However, this self-directed learning journey is fraught with challenges, chief among them being the prevalence of financial misinformation. While a vast knowledge repository, the internet also serves as a breeding ground for erroneous financial advice and strategies. For instance, young adults might come across misleading "get rich quick" schemes or investment "tips" that promise high returns with little risk, which are not only unrealistic but also potentially dangerous. Additionally, the complex jargon of financial literature can be another barrier, leading to misinterpretations and misapplications of sound financial strategies.

Even when accurate and reliable information is obtained, implementing it into daily life is another hurdle. Many young adults struggle with the discipline required to apply financial knowledge consistently. The psychological barriers, such as fear of taking risks, procrastination, or even the cognitive bias that one's current habits are sufficient, prevent the practical application of sound financial principles. Furthermore, lifestyle inflation—increasing one's spending as income rises—can negate the benefits of financial planning and saving, leaving individuals no better off than before.

I invested $10,000 in gold and silver at age 19. Two years later, my money doubled. I thought that I was a young Warren Buffet. Never mind that the only reason I even thought about investing in those commodities was because my parents were investing in them. But there I was, an investing genius. Having made such a wise and mature decision, it only made sense to continue that trend. So, I took that money and invested it all in a 4-year-old Chevy Silverado. Now, not only was I a genius, but I also had proof that I was. Over the next few years, I continued to invest in that truck as I had to replace the ball bearings and arms on the front end a couple of times, roughly $2,000 each time. Add depreciation to those figures, and I had found a mine, a land mine.

This gap between knowledge acquisition and practical application highlights a critical disconnect contributing to ongoing financial instability. Addressing this requires not just education but also mentoring and support systems to help young adults navigate the complexities of financial management effectively.

3

Evolving Economics

In the labyrinth of personal finance, not all factors are within your control. This chapter delves into the evolving economic forces that, despite your best efforts, can impact your financial success. Understanding these elements isn't about making excuses but recognizing the playing field and strategizing accordingly.

COVID-19: A Test of Financial Resilience

The COVID-19 pandemic served as an unprecedented global challenge that tested the financial stability of businesses and individuals alike. As economies worldwide were brought to a standstill, many companies faced severe disruptions—some temporary, others permanent. The sudden loss of income and the uncertainty of the future placed immense strain on financial systems, businesses, and personal finances.

However, the pandemic also highlighted the critical importance of having a robust financial plan. Those with emergency funds, diversified income streams, and flexible financial plans were better equipped to withstand the economic shocks. Personal savings acted as a buffer against the sudden loss of employment or reduced income, providing essential financial breathing room during lockdowns and restrictions.

Businesses that had set aside contingency funds or had access to emergency lines of credit could manage cash flows more effectively when their operations were disrupted. Furthermore, individuals and businesses that were quick to adapt to the new economic environment—by shifting to online platforms, finding alternative delivery methods, or modifying their services to meet new consumer needs—often found new opportunities amidst the crisis. There are always opportunities for those who are looking for them.

This subsection of the pandemic's economic impact is a potent reminder of why financial preparedness is crucial. It underscores the necessity of planning for the unexpected and maintaining financial flexibility to adapt to rapid changes. The lessons learned from navigating the pandemic can guide future financial strategies, ensuring greater resilience against unforeseen events.

Inflation

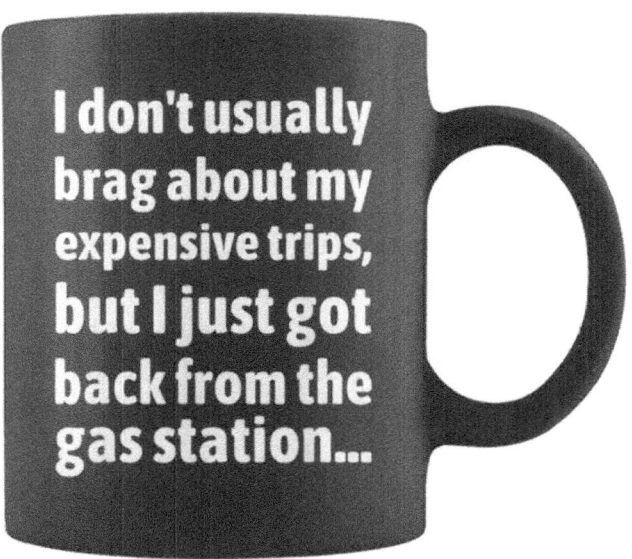

Having been more influenced by the recent pandemic than in the few years previous, inflation is the stealthy giant that erodes purchasing power over time. As prices for goods and services rise, the value of money falls, meaning today's dollar will buy less in the future. This inevitable economic phenomenon affects everyone, but its impact is most pronounced on those who fail to plan for it. While you can't stop inflation, you can mitigate its effects by investing in assets that traditionally outpace inflation, such as stocks, real estate, or commodities. Knowledge and proactive financial planning are your best defenses against this relentless economic force.

Raises at Work to Keep Up with Inflation

Ideally, annual raises at work should align with or exceed the inflation rate to help you maintain your purchasing power. However, the reality often falls short. Many sectors and companies do not automatically adjust wages based on inflationary pressures. This disconnect means that even with hard work and dedication, your salary may not keep pace with the rising cost of living, straining your financial stability. Recognizing this gap is crucial, not for resignation but for empowerment, prompting you to seek additional income sources or negotiate better wages.

I firmly believe that the majority of the time, you will continue to receive the average raise unless you ask. Like any other company, your employer is running a business, and the main goal is keeping expenses as low as possible. Even if you are the favorite employee, it doesn't always mean you will receive as much as you think you should. Having said that, and this will be covered more in the next chapter, you aren't entitled to anything more than what your employer seems fair. It's their business. However, you can increase your odds by working hard, being willing to help and do a little extra, being kind, and showing gratitude for being employed. If, after having done this, you feel you are being undervalued, and a better opportunity comes along, take it. Remember, it's nothing personal, just business.

Now, if you want to have more control of your destiny, you have to own something. This is no easy task, especially since the majority of businesses fail within the first five years. However, it can be much easier and less risky today with more and more things transferring from brick and mortar to online. This doesn't mean quitting your job and starting a business, but it can be a combination of the two. More and more people have side hustles and fund them from the income earned from their jobs.

The Enticing Marketing of 'Buy Now, Pay Later'

In an era of instant gratification, "buy now, pay later" marketing strategies are particularly seductive. These offers, while appealing, encourage spending beyond one's means, leading to debt accumulation that can outpace one's ability to repay. This tactic exploits the common desire for immediate ownership, often sidelining the financial implications. While these services offer convenience and immediate satisfaction, they can derail financial stability if not managed with strict discipline and a clear understanding of terms and conditions. Understand that if you can't afford it now, it's probably best not to purchase it, thinking you can afford it in the ensuing months when payment comes due.

By recognizing these uncontrollable economic elements, you are better equipped to navigate the financial challenges they pose. This understanding allows you to plan strategically, ensuring that while you may not control these factors, they do not control you, either. Let's arm ourselves with this knowledge and forge a path to financial resilience despite the challenges.

4

Social and Political Pressure

Navigating the treacherous waters of personal finance is daunting enough without the added whirlpools of social and political pressures. This chapter explores how these influences can distort your financial perspective, often pushing you towards decisions that sabotage long-term stability. Understanding these pressures isn't about assigning blame—it's about arming yourself with awareness and choosing to act differently.

Personal Circle Influence

The saying "You are the average of the five people you spend the most time with" holds significant weight regarding financial habits. A circle of friends that splurges without thought and handles money irresponsibly can drag you down the same path. Conversely, surrounding yourself with financially savvy and responsible individuals can elevate your own financial behaviors. These friends can introduce you to better habits, more robust planning strategies, and a supportive environment conducive to financial growth. Choosing your social circle wisely is not just a matter of social comfort but financial health. Great minds think alike, while poor minds don't think at all.

Though negative and irresponsible, cutting the cord with your current social circle can be difficult. After all, they are your friends, right? But that is precisely what needs to happen if you plan to excel.

You may be aware of this little phenomenon about what happens with a bucket of crabs. Fishermen do not have to put a lid on the bucket because just as one crab is about to crest the rim, the other crabs grab it and pull it back into the bucket. Similarly, as weird as it may sound, those with a negative attitude often do not like to watch others succeed because they begin to realize that they are still in the bucket and don't really plan to get out. This may cause them to have feelings of insecurity, shame, or guilt. So, it only makes sense to pull those who are trying to improve their situation back down into the bucket. Put it this way. If those in your current social circle genuinely are friends, they will help push you up rather than drag you back down.

YOLO (You Only Live Once) Mentality

The "YOLO" mentality, a modern mantra for living in the moment, often justifies reckless spending under the guise of making the most of the present. While seizing the day is vital, neglecting future consequences, especially financial ones, can lead to serious repercussions. Overspending today without a plan for tomorrow can quickly spiral into debt and financial insecurity. Balancing enjoyment of life with prudent financial planning is essential, ensuring that living for today doesn't compromise your financial future.

Entitlement

In today's political climate, the notion of entitlement—expecting certain benefits or resources without corresponding efforts—can seep into personal financial attitudes. This mindset undermines the fundamental principles of hard work and earning one's way. Recognizing and resisting the allure of entitlement is crucial, as it can lead to frustration and stagnation when the expected financial support does not materialize or is withdrawn.

This mindset is increasing, making it much more difficult not to fall in line with the masses. It could be that one of the underlying factors of entitlement is status. No one wants to be viewed as a failure, so why not blame the situation on someone or something else and demand compensation for the inconvenience? This coincides with having a good social group and taking ownership.

Lack of Accountability

Government policies, like loan bailouts, while designed to provide relief, can sometimes promote a lack of individual accountability. These measures can create expectations that debts or poor financial decisions will be mitigated by external help, reducing the incentive for personal financial discipline. While such policies are crucial safety nets during economic crises, relying on them can inhibit the development of robust financial habits necessary for long-term stability.

This chapter calls for a mindful examination of how social circles, societal messages, and political climates influence your financial decisions. By understanding and adjusting to these pressures, you can forge a path to financial success that is both responsible and sustainable. Let's move forward with this knowledge, ready to take on the next challenge: finding your way out of financial despair.

5

The Way Out of Financial Despair

Breaking free from financial despair requires both a change in mindset and practical steps towards better financial health. Whether you've been too passive or struggling despite your best efforts, this chapter offers concrete strategies to revitalize your financial situation and mindset. It's time to roll up your sleeves and commit to a financial recovery and success journey.

Make a Plan and Set Goals

The first step out of financial despair is to define where you want to go. Set clear, achievable goals—whether it's paying off debt, saving for a house, or building an emergency fund. Visualize your financial dreams and break them down into measurable steps. This roadmap will not only guide your daily decisions but also keep you motivated. Remember, goals are dreams with deadlines, so set specific timelines for each milestone.

Humans are visual. Put your goals in front of you where you see them daily. Rather than just keeping your goals in written form, find and print or cut out photos/images that depict what you want to achieve. Put these up on your walls or mirrors. If you haven't heard the term before, this is called a vision board. Of the successful entrepreneurs using vision boards, 76% announced that the success they were seeing was in alignment with those items on their vision boards, according to a TD Bank survey.

Imagery is powerful. Take time to imagine yourself having already achieved your goals. Allow your mind and emotions of that accomplishment to take hold of you. This exercise will be a great addition to your vision boards. Think this is weird and just a hoax? Try it for 5-10 minutes every day for two weeks and see if it doesn't put you in a more optimistic and focused mindset to accomplish your goals. I can't say that I wasn't doubtful when I was encouraged to try it, but I did it. Did my mind wonder about other things? Sure did. Did I doze off a little bit? Yep. But I kept at it, and it became easier and more helpful.

Create a Budget to Get Out of Debt

Debt can be overwhelming, but escaping it is possible with the right plan. Create a detailed budget that tracks every dollar earned and spent. Free budget worksheets can be found online if you don't already have one. Know that poor spending habits, such as eating out often, could be the real reason and cause of your financial hardship rather than how much you earn. Prioritize expenses, cut unnecessary costs, and allocate extra funds to paying off debts fastest to slowest or highest interest to lowest. This disciplined approach is your most powerful tool in regaining financial control. Dave Ramsey's "7 Baby Steps" process can be a great starting point if you don't know where to begin.

Change Group of Closest Friends

As previously discussed, the company you keep can significantly influence your financial behaviors. If your current friends encourage frivolous spending or lack financial ambitions, it might be time to seek new associations. Align yourself with people who embody financial wisdom and positivity. Their habits, mindset, and support can inspire and propel you towards your own financial goals.

Work Hard

The principle of hard work cannot be overstated when escaping financial despair. This isn't merely about clocking in extra hours at your job; it's about proactively seeking opportunities to advance your financial goals. Working hard means continuously striving to improve your skills, seeking promotions or better job opportunities, and sometimes, juggling multiple income streams. It also involves educating yourself about financial markets and investment opportunities that can grow your wealth over time.

For those who feel stuck or need a clear upward trajectory in their current roles, working hard might mean retraining for a different field with higher earning potential or starting a side business that aligns with personal passions or market needs. The goal is to create a robust financial base that covers your current lifestyle and fuels your future dreams and ambitions. Remember, the fruits of hard work are not instant, but they compound over time, leading to lasting financial security and independence.

Give to Others

While it may seem counterintuitive when facing financial difficulties, giving to others can be vital in building a sound financial and personal life. The act of giving—whether it's financial aid, volunteering time, or sharing resources—can enrich your life by building deeper connections with your community and expanding your network. These relationships can often open doors to new opportunities and collaborations that wouldn't have been available otherwise.

Moreover, giving promotes a positive mindset and can improve emotional and psychological well-being. It shifts focus from one's own financial struggles and fosters gratitude for what one already has. This perspective is vital for maintaining motivation and perseverance in overcoming financial obstacles.

Financial giving should be strategic and within your means, ensuring it doesn't compromise your financial recovery. This could be as simple as donating a small percentage of your income to a cause you care about or offering your skills to help others without financial exchange. As the adage goes, what goes around comes around. By putting goodwill into the world, you set the stage for reciprocal benefits that often manifest in both expected and unexpected ways, contributing to your overall financial resilience and success.

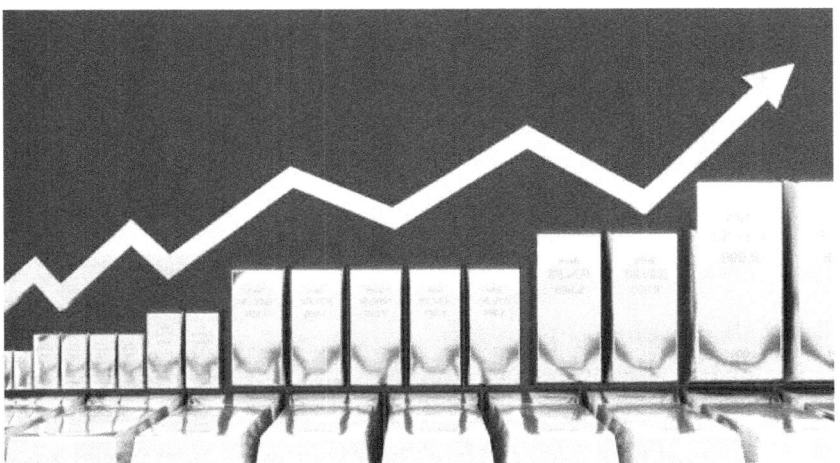

Initial Steps and Benefits of Investing

Investing is one of the most effective ways to build wealth over time, and getting started earlier can significantly amplify its benefits due to the power of compound interest. The first step in investing is understanding different investment options and how they fit into your financial goals. Establishing an emergency fund first is crucial to ensure you can afford to invest without prematurely withdrawing funds.

Common Investing Accounts

Some of the most common investment accounts include:

1. 401(k) or 403(b) Plans - These are employer-sponsored retirement plans that allow you to invest a portion of your paycheck before taxes are taken out. Many employers offer a matching contribution up to a certain percentage, which can significantly boost your savings.
2. Individual Retirement Accounts (IRAs) - There are two main types of IRAs: Traditional and Roth. Both offer tax advantages that can help you save for retirement but differ in the tax treatment of contributions and withdrawals.
3. Brokerage Accounts - Unlike 401(k)s and IRAs, brokerage accounts don't have specific tax advantages for retirement, but they offer more flexibility in investment choices and access to your funds.
4. Education Savings Accounts (ESAs) or 529 Plans - These accounts offer tax-free growth and withdrawals when the funds are used to pay for qualified education expenses.

Example of Compound Interest

To illustrate the power of compound interest, consider a scenario where you start investing $100 per month at the age of 20, with an average annual return of 7%. Here's how your investment would grow over the years:

- Age 30: You would have contributed $12,000, but your investment would be worth approximately $17,000 thanks to compound interest.
- Age 40: Your total contributions would amount to $24,000, but your investment would have grown to around $50,000.
- Age 50: Having contributed $36,000, your account balance would

be about $113,000.
- Age 60: After 40 years of investing a total of $48,000, your balance would be approximately $240,000.

These figures demonstrate how regular investments, even in small amounts, can grow significantly over time due to the effects of compounding. This example underscores the importance of starting to invest as early as possible and maintaining consistent contributions to maximize the growth potential of your investments.

Recommended Reading

To further equip yourself, here are a few of my favorite books that have helped me along the way and will provide more context and backup to the principles discussed throughout this book. I've included a couple of quotes from each. These will expand your understanding of finances, mindset, and goal setting:

"The Richest Man in Babylon" by George S. Clason - This book provides financial advice through a collection of parables set in ancient Babylon, focusing on the basics of saving, investing, and financial planning.

- "If you have not acquired more than a bare existence in the years since we were youths, it is because you either have failed to learn the laws that govern the building of wealth, or else you do not observe them."
- "To attract good luck to oneself, it is necessary to take advantage of opportunities."

"Rich Dad Poor Dad" by Robert Kiyosaki - This book contrasts the differing financial philosophies of Kiyosaki's own father and his friend's father, offering insights into how wealth is built and maintained through investing, owning businesses, and avoiding conventional financial wisdom.

- "The poor and the middle class work for money. The rich have money work for them."
- "If people are prepared to be flexible, keep an open mind and learn, they will grow richer and richer despite tough changes. If they think money will solve problems, they will have a rough ride. Intelligence solves problems and produces money. Money without financial intelligence is money soon gone."

"Mindset" by Carol S. Dweck - Dweck explains how our success in virtually every area of life can be influenced by how we think about our talents and abilities, introducing the concept of a fixed mindset versus a growth mindset.

- "For thirty years, my research has shown that the view you adopt for yourself profoundly affects the way you lead your life. It can determine whether you become the person you want to be and whether you accomplish the things you value."
- "In one world, effort is a bad thing. It, like failure, means you're not smart or talented. If you were, you wouldn't need effort. In the other world, effort is what *makes* you smart or talented."

"The One Thing" by Gary Keller and Jay Papasan - This book argues that focusing on your most important task can dramatically improve your productivity and success rate, emphasizing the power of prioritizing.

- "It's not that we have too little time to do all the things we need to do, it's that we feel the need to do too many things in the time we have."

- "You don't need to be a disciplined person to be successful. In fact, you can become successful with less discipline than you think, for one simple reason: success is about doing the right thing, not about doing everything right."

"The Power of the Other" by Dr. Henry Cloud - Dr. Cloud examines the profound impact that our connections with others have on our performance and well-being, stressing the importance of building healthy relationships.

- "We are fueled from the outside, from connection with others. Whether it's a smartphone or a human, when the system can't make a connection, it begins to run down. This is an indisputable reality. Humans need connection, and their systems are always searching for one."
- "In the more than twenty-five years I've been working with high-powered CEOs and other top performers, one characteristic stands out: the leaders who accomplish the most, thrive the most, overcome the most are *not afraid to say they need help.*"

"The Go-Giver" by Bob Burg and John David Mann - This business parable champions the idea that the secret to success is giving, advocating for a generous approach in business and life to unlock true fulfillment and success.

- "In fact, most people just laugh when they hear that the secret to success is *giving.* […] Then again, most people are nowhere near as successful as they wish they were."
- "Because if you place the other person's interest first, your interests will always be taken care of. Always. Some people call it enlightened self-interest. Watch out for what other people need, with the faith

that when you do, you'll get what you need."

There are many more books I could reference, but the list has to end somewhere. Each of these resources offers unique perspectives and strategies to reinforce the financial principles and practices outlined in this chapter. With these tools, hard work, and the right mindset, your path out of financial despair is not just a possibility—it's a certainty.

6

Conclusion

As we draw the curtains on this journey through the tangled financial landscape many young adults face today, it's essential to reflect on the insights and strategies discussed. From recognizing the educational gaps in financial literacy to understanding the economic and social pressures that shape your financial world, this book has aimed to equip you with the knowledge and tools necessary for financial resilience.

You've been presented with practical steps to overcome financial despair, strategies to navigate through the ever-evolving economic challenges, and ways to adjust your social dynamics to foster better financial health. Remember, the path to financial freedom is built on discipline, informed decision-making, and continuous personal growth.

Now, it's your turn to take action. Apply what you've learned, adjust your strategies as needed, and keep moving towards your financial goals. The principles outlined in this book are not just theories but actionable steps that can lead to real change if implemented diligently and consistently.

Remember, every step you take is a step towards financial independence. Keep pushing forward, keep learning, and never hesitate to seek new strategies to propel you even further. Your financial freedom isn't just a dream—it's a future you can build with persistence and the right mindset.

As you progress on your financial journey, your experiences and successes can inspire and guide others. I encourage you to share your story and how this book has impacted your financial outlook. Please take a moment to leave a review on Amazon. Your feedback helps us improve and serves as a beacon for others navigating their own financial challenges.

7

Resources

OpenAI. (2021). ChatGPT (GPT-4) [Software]. OpenAI. https://www.openai.com/

Burg, B., & Mann, J. D. (2010). *The Go-Giver: A Little Story About a Powerful Business Idea*. Penguin UK.

Clason, G. S. (2013). *The richest man in Babylon: George S. Clason's Bestselling Guide to Financial Success: Saving Money and Putting It to Work for You by Clason, George S. , Parable, Babylonian (2013) Paperback*. Createspace Independent Publishing Platform.

Cloud, H. (2016). *The power of the other: The startling effect other people have on you, from the boardroom to the bedroom and beyond-and what to do about it*. HarperCollins.

Dweck, C. S. (2007). *Mindset: The New Psychology of Success*. Ballantine Books.

Keller, G., & Papasan, J. (2013). *The ONE thing: The Surprisingly Simple Truth Behind Extraordinary Results*. Bard Press.

Kiyosaki, R. T. (2015). *Rich dad poor dad: What the Rich Teach Their Kids about Money— that the Poor and Middle Class Do Not!*

Luthi, B., Pentis, A., & Lowery, K. (2024, January 23). What is the average student loan debt in 2024 — and what are the impacts? *CNN*

Underscored Money. https://www.cnn.com/cnn-underscored/money/average-student-loan-debt#:~:text=The%20average%20student%20loan%20debt%20for%20bachelor's%20degree%20recipients%20was,the%20three%20national%20credit%20bureaus

McNair, K. (2023, April 14). 18 states require personal finance education in schools—here's what they're teaching kids about money. *CNBC*. https://www.cnbc.com/2023/04/13/how-personal-finance-is-taught-in-us-schools.html

Melore, C. (2021, January 13). Are you financially literate? Most parents wish they knew more about money growing up. *Study Finds*. https://studyfinds.org/financially-literate-most-parents-wish-they-knew-more-about-money-childhood/

Nguyen, J. (2022, December 20). *Money and millennials: The cost of living in 2022 vs. 1972*. Marketplace. https://www.marketplace.org/2022/08/17/money-and-millennials-the-cost-of-living-in-2022-vs-1972/

Travers, M. (2024, March 30). A psychologist explains the power of 'Vision boarding' for success. *Forbes*. https://www.forbes.com/sites/traversmark/2024/03/29/a-psychologist-explains-the-power-of-vision-boarding-for-success/?sh=4dd5cf024e69

www.ingramcontent.com/pod-product-compliance
Lightning Source LLC
Chambersburg PA
CBHW050250230526
45470CB00005B/2205